CALLIGRAPHY

The Diagram Group

BROCKHAMPTON
DIAGRAM
GUIDES

Calligraphy

© Diagram Visual Information Ltd. 1997
  195 Kentish Town Road
  London
  NW5 2JU

All rights reserved including the right of reproduction in whole or in part in any form

First published in Great Britain in 1997 by
Brockhampton Press Ltd
20 Bloomsbury Street
London
WC1 2QA
a member of the Hodder Headline Group PLC

ISBN 1-86019-742-6

Also in this series:
Card Games
How the Body Works
Identifying Architecture
Kings and Queens of Britain
Magic Tricks
Party Games
Soccer Skills

Introduction

Calligraphy is the craft of writing beautifully. It will take time and patience before you acquire the range of skills which are the hallmark of a good calligrapher.

This practical guide provides a programme of clear instruction for someone beginning calligraphy. There are exercises, informative diagrams and a step-by-step account of techniques to help you practise and improve your penmanship.

The first section of the book describes basic tools and materials – pens, nibs, inks, paints and types of paper. Simple letterforms are explained and illustrated in the second section, and in the third we show you how to master the techniques of spacing, centring and layout.

Good calligraphy comes through practice and patience. In this book we aim to show you how practising calligraphy can be fun and rewarding. Once you have learned the basic letterforms and practised the various techniques you can begin to experiment with different lettering styles. Eventually you will learn to apply styles which help to express the subject matter of the text.

Contents

6	Basic tools
12	Letterforms
38	Techniques

Basic tools

The most basic tools in calligraphy are your hand and eyes. Coordinating their use to produce letters that are well spaced and attractive will require practice and dedication. Exercises and techniques for developing your writing skills are given in sections 2 and 3.

In this section we describe the equipment you will need to begin calligraphy. There are illustrations of the main types of pen and other writing tools, with an indication of the effects that can be achieved with each type.

Besides pens, paper and ink you will need a comfortable place to work, preferably one with the maximum of natural light. You will also need a sturdy flat surface on which to rest your drawing board and plenty of storage space for your equipment and work.

TAKING CARE OF YOUR EQUIPMENT

It is good practice to clean pens and brushes immediately after use. This will help to lengthen their useful life, and you are more likely to practise lettering in a spare moment if your equipment is already clean.

Always keep pencils sharp and ready to use.

Your writing tools should be kept in a safe place where they are unlikely to become damaged. Do not allow others to use them.

PREPARING A WRITING BOARD

PREPARING A WRITING BOARD

If you do not have a writing board, you can make a simple one as follows:
1 Find a strong, flat board with straight edges. Prop it up at an angle of 30° using bricks or books. Make sure it is firm.
2 Tape three sheets of thick paper securely to the board to create a smooth writing surface.
3 Using masking tape, fix a piece of paper with ruled lines underneath your writing paper; the lines, visible through the writing paper, will provide a guide for your writing.
4 Your writing hand should remain level throughout so make sure that the writing paper can be moved upwards when you reach the bottom of the page. If you need to secure the paper to stop it moving use only a small amount of tape which can easily be removed.
5 Use a sheet of layout paper to protect the part of the writing paper you are not using from grease and ink splatters.

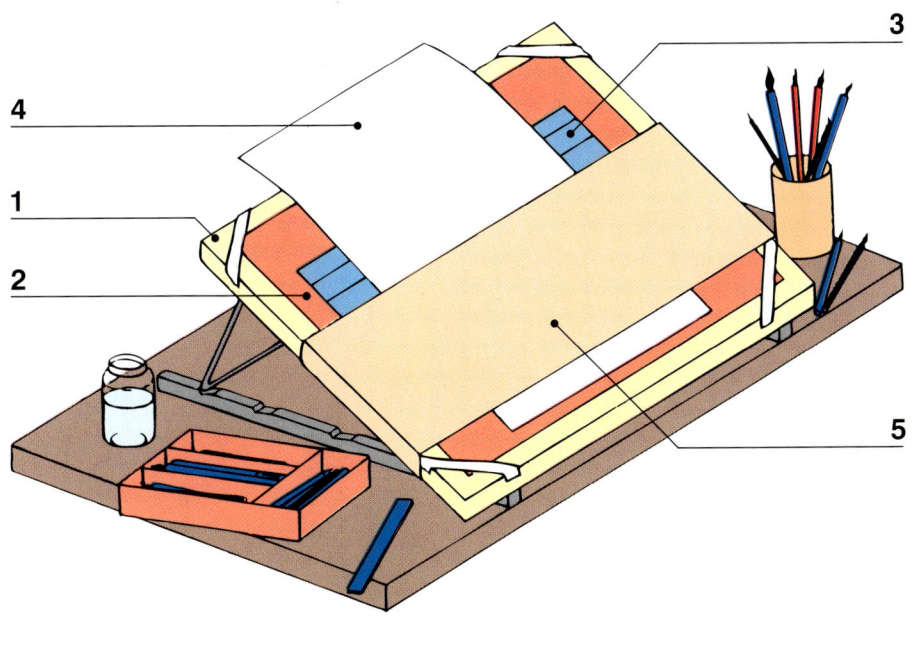

BASIC TOOLS

PENS AND WRITING TOOLS

A variety of writing implements can be used in calligraphy. Some of the most popular are as follows:

1 An instant marker pen, available in a variety of widths and colours. It is ideal for practising and planning layouts.
2 A felt tip pen, available in many widths and colours (a wedge-tipped pen is illustrated). It is good for practising and planning layouts.
3 A fine tip pen is useful for ruling-up templates (see pages 38–39).
4 A carpenter's pencil is handy for practising and experimenting with different layouts.
5 A double pencil is useful for showing letter construction. Simply bind two pencils together at the top and bottom with tape or rubber bands. To make a broader pen, place an eraser between the two pencils and then bind them together. If you

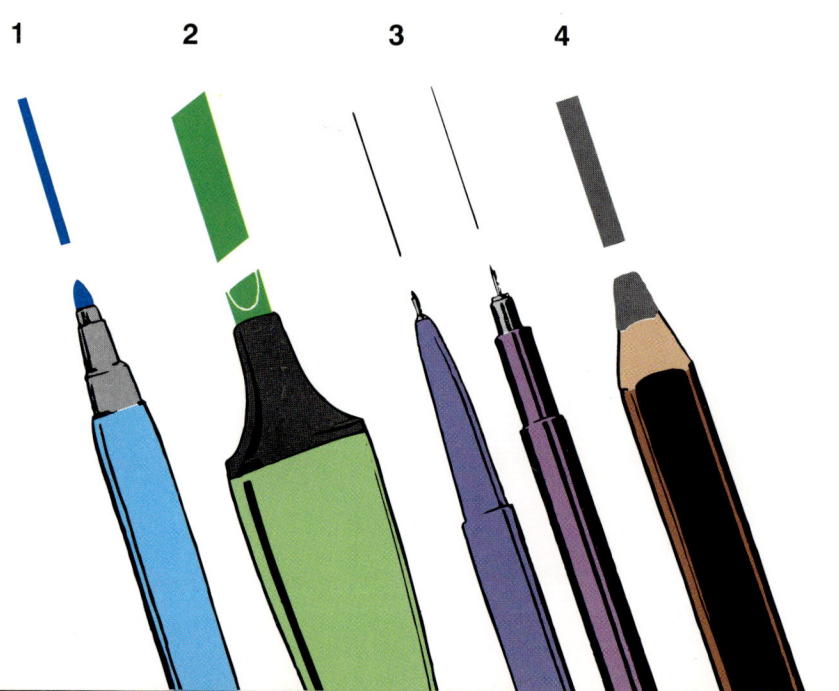

PENS AND WRITING TOOLS

want a narrower pen, shave off some of the wood from the length of the pencils before binding.

6 A chisel-ended felt tip pen can be made by cutting small wedges out of the tip of a wedge-tipped pen with a scalpel. It produces a decorative mark.

7 A reed pen can be made from bamboo, honeysuckle or other tubular stems. It is the original broad-nibbed pen and is ideal for large letters.

8 A synthetic 'reed pen' can be made from a piece of nylon tubing (available from hardware stores) by cutting the tube at one end to form a nib.

9 A quill is made from a cured flight feather of a goose or swan. The feather is shaped at the end with a sharp knife.

10 A William Mitchell Roundhand nib with a slip-on reservoir. Note that reservoirs holding a supply of ink can also be attached to the shafts of pens **7**, **8** and **9**. A pen with a reservoir does not need to be dipped into the ink pot after every stroke.

BASIC TOOLS

ADDITIONAL MATERIALS

Nibs
As well as selecting a writing implement, you must also consider the size and style of pen nib. Nibs either come already attached to the pen shaft or they can be bought separately. You should aim to have a range of good quality nibs of different widths. Each manufacturer uses a different numbering system to indicate the size of the nib. You should familiarize yourself with the ranges of styles and sizes available.

Inks
When choosing ink always make sure it is non-waterproof; waterproof inks contain gum which will clog your pen. ● Ordinary permanent black fountain pen ink is best to start off with. ● Black Indian ink is good for finished work as it is dense and very black. ● Calligraphy ink is specially formulated for use with all kinds of pens; it gives a dense black finish. ● There are many other types

Paper
You will probably use a great deal of paper so find a good art shop or specialist paper supplier where you can stock up regularly. Good paper is worth paying extra for, but only buy small quantities until you find a paper you like. Three main factors to consider when choosing paper are: weight (thickness), surface texture ('tooth') and finish (absorbency). Experiment with different paper, ink and pen combinations. When you try a new type of paper, write the name and other details in a corner so that you can easily reorder if you find you like it. ● To begin with, buy an A3 layout pad. This is an inexpensive, translucent, lightweight paper which can be used for practice and pasting-up. Ruled guidelines placed underneath it will show through. ● Good quality drawing paper is very useful so try a few different weights, then stock up with ones you like.

ADDITIONAL MATERIALS

and colours of ink available for you to experiment with. Always secure your ink bottles to the table to avoid spillage.

Paint

Give a new dimension to your work by using paints. ● An opaque finish can be obtained with gouache paints (non-translucent watercolours). Useful colours to start off with are: zinc (Chinese) white, cobalt blue, lemon yellow, emerald oxide of chromium (mix in lemon yellow to give it body) and spectrum red or vermilion hue. ● If you already have watercolours you can add zinc white to give opacity to your letters. ● For preparing paint you need a mixing dish and a dropper bottle filled with water. Add water to the paint drop by drop. During a long piece of work you will need to add water to compensate for evaporation. ● Use old cheap brushes for mixing and transferring paint from the mixing dish to the nib. If the brushes have long handles, shorten them to prevent accidents.

● Parch marque is a substitute for parchment and is ideal for making a finished piece look interesting. ● Fabriano paper, made from cotton, comes in several weights and is very good to use.

Paper sizes

SIZE	METRIC	IMPERIAL	NEAREST US EQUIVALENTS
A5	148 x 210 mm	5⁷/₈ x 8¹/₄ in	5¹/₂ x 8¹/₂ in
A4	210 x 297 mm	8¹/₄ x 11³/₄ in	8¹/₂ x 11 in; 9 x 12 in
A3	297 x 420 mm	11³/₄ x 16¹/₂ in	11 x 14 in; 14 x 17 in; 11 x 17 in; 12 x 18 in
A2	420 x 594 mm	16¹/₂ x 23¹/₂ in	18 x 24 in; 19 x 24 in

Letterforms

The alphabet we know today has two basic forms – capitals or upper case letters (majuscules) and lower case letters (minuscules). The letterform is the 'hand' or style in which you write letters of the alphabet. In this section we describe three letterforms which if practised will give you a firm grounding in calligraphy. The skeleton letterform is the most basic style of the upper and lower case alphabets. Skeleton letters do not rely on the 'thick and thin' effect of a broad-nibbed pen; the letters can be made as large or as small, or as thick or thin as you wish. The other two letterforms described in this chapter – Foundational and Italic – will require a broad-nibbed pen.

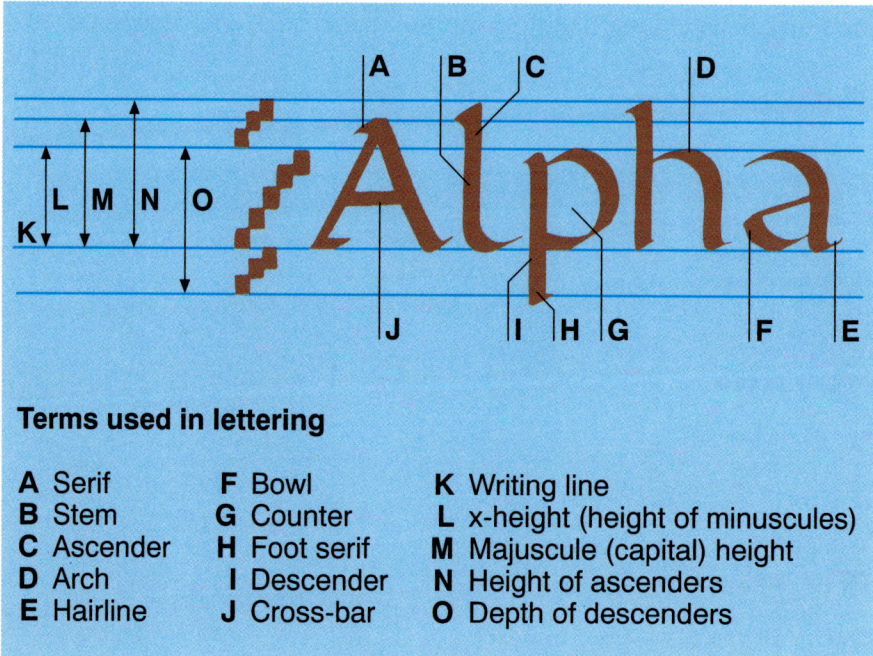

Terms used in lettering

- **A** Serif
- **B** Stem
- **C** Ascender
- **D** Arch
- **E** Hairline
- **F** Bowl
- **G** Counter
- **H** Foot serif
- **I** Descender
- **J** Cross-bar
- **K** Writing line
- **L** x-height (height of minuscules)
- **M** Majuscule (capital) height
- **N** Height of ascenders
- **O** Depth of descenders

LETTERFORM PROPORTIONS

Ladders

The height of each letterform is set at a specific number of nib widths. For example, Foundational majuscules (**A**) are 6 nib widths high and the minuscules are 4½ nib widths high. Italic majuscules (**B**) are 7 nib widths high and the minuscules are 5. You can check that your lettering is the correct height by using your nib as a measure. Hold the pen at a pen angle of 90° (*see below*), then measure the correct number of nib widths by drawing a series of pen marks in a formation known as a ladder. You must make a new ladder each time you use a different size of nib or change lettering style. This will ensure that your letters are always in the correct proportions for the lettering style and nib size.

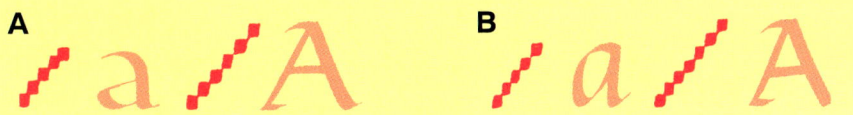

Guidelines

Guidelines are ruled lines which help you to draw letters in the correct proportions. They are either fine pencil lines ruled on the writing sheet itself or lines on a template placed underneath the writing sheet and which show through the paper. Once you know the set heights for a particular letterform you can draw guidelines by making a ladder and ruling pencil lines from the ladder.

Pen angles

The pen angle is the angle between the flat edge of the nib and the horizontal writing line. Different letterforms require different pen angles.

SKELETON LETTERS

The skeleton alphabet is the first lettering style to learn. It is the most basic form of the alphabet and has no thick or thin strokes. For this reason it can be made with any monoline pen (any pen with a round nib). The x-height of the minuscules (lower case letters) should be half the height of the majuscules (upper case letters); the height of the ascenders should equal the height of the

SKELETON LETTERS

majuscules. Numerals are formed slightly higher or lower than the x-height. When you practise drawing skeleton letters, keep in mind that they are all based on combinations of the straight line and the circle. Follow the stroke order indicated in the diagrams below for a smoother outline. To practise drawing the majuscules, divide them into four groups based on their relative shapes and draw each one using squared paper (see overleaf). This way you will learn how one skeleton letter differs from the next.

LETTERFORMS

SHAPE AND SPACE

Proportional groups

1. C D G O Q are based on a circle. D and G use the edge of a rectangle.
2. A H N T U V X Y Z all fit into a rectangle. Note that the crossbars on A and H are at different heights.
3. B E F J K L P R S use half a square. Curves in the lower section need to be a fraction larger to stop letters looking top-heavy.
4. M fits into a square. W (double V, not double U!) is the widest letter; I is the narrowest.

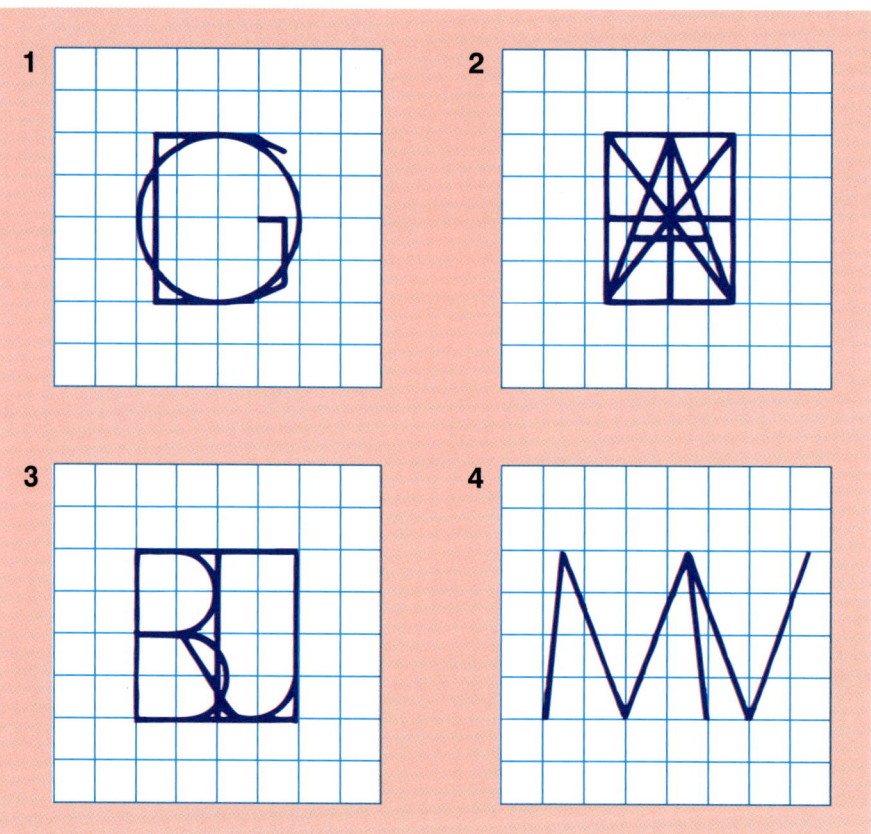

SHAPE AND SPACE

Letter spacing

The skeleton alphabet is ideal for practising letter spacing because its simplicity allows faults to become obvious. The most important thing to remember is to take the shape of the adjoining letters into account. The following hints for creating well-balanced lettering apply to all letterforms:

1 Leave a large gap between two verticals.
2 Vertical and round letters should be positioned closer together.
3 Two round letters should be positioned even closer together.
4 Regular spacing (i.e. leaving the same gap between each letter) leads to unbalanced lettering.
5 Balanced letters are irregularly spaced.

THE FOUNDATIONAL HAND

The Foundational hand is the name given by the calligrapher and typographer Edward Johnston to the style he developed in the early years of this century. Based on his study of the Ramsay Psalter, a 10th-century Carolingian manuscript in the British Museum, it shares the proportions and balance of the manuscript's letters. The Foundational minuscule alphabet is shown on this and the next page; the majuscule alphabet, which is based on classic Roman capitals, is shown on pages 22 and 23.

THE FOUNDATIONAL HAND

r s t u v w x y z

g x y y 1 2 3 4

5 6 7 8 9 0

MINUSCULE AND MAJUSCULE SIZES

The minuscules have an x-height of $4\frac{1}{2}$ nib widths, with an ascender height of 7 nib widths; the majuscule height is 6 nib widths. The letters stand vertically without a slope and their basic shape is a round O. They are written with the pen and nib at an angle of 30° to the writing line, except in a few cases where different pen angles must be used (see minuscule diagonals on the page opposite and majuscule pen angles on page 24).

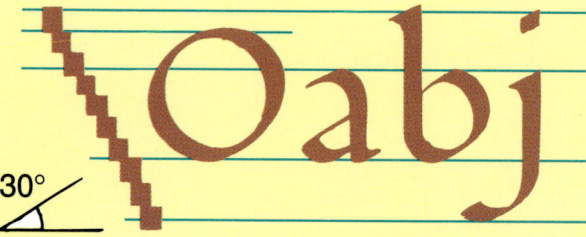

Minuscule letter groups

Foundational hand minuscules are grouped according to some basic shapes. It is best to learn one basic shape at a time by practising the letters from each group separately.

Group 1: the O shape Following the stroke order given in the diagram on pages 18 and 19, the O shape is drawn from the 11 o'clock to the 5 o'clock position, first anticlockwise and then clockwise.

1

MINUSCULE AND MAJUSCULE SIZES

Group 2: the arch shape Note how it relates to the O shape and has no angularity.

Group 3: the inverted arch, the u shape The curved bases of l and t match the curve of the letter u.

Group 4: diagonals The pen angle is steepened for these strokes, otherwise the letters would spread too wide.

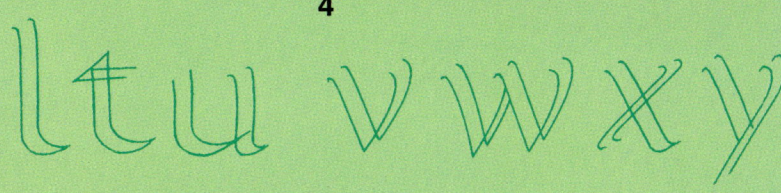

Group 5: the remaining letters The shapes of these letters have little in common; all need individual attention during construction.

THE FOUNDATIONAL MAJUSCULES

The Foundational hand majuscule alphabet is a modern version of the classic Roman capitals alphabet which has been adapted for the use of the broad-nibbed pen. The original Roman capitals, for example those seen on Trajan's Column in Rome, aimed to convey

THE FOUNDATIONAL MAJUSCULES

the power of the Roman Empire. They were drawn with a brush before being cut in stone with a chisel. These capitals have inspired letter cutters, typographers and signwriters for two thousand years and their elegance has been captured in the modern pen version. The majuscules and minuscules of the Foundational hand make up one of the most popular letterforms used by calligraphers.

Majuscule pen angles

The pen angle is 30°, but there are a few exceptions to this. Diagonal strokes are steepened to 45°, and occasionally the pen is flattened to a mere 5° to maintain a harmonious look.

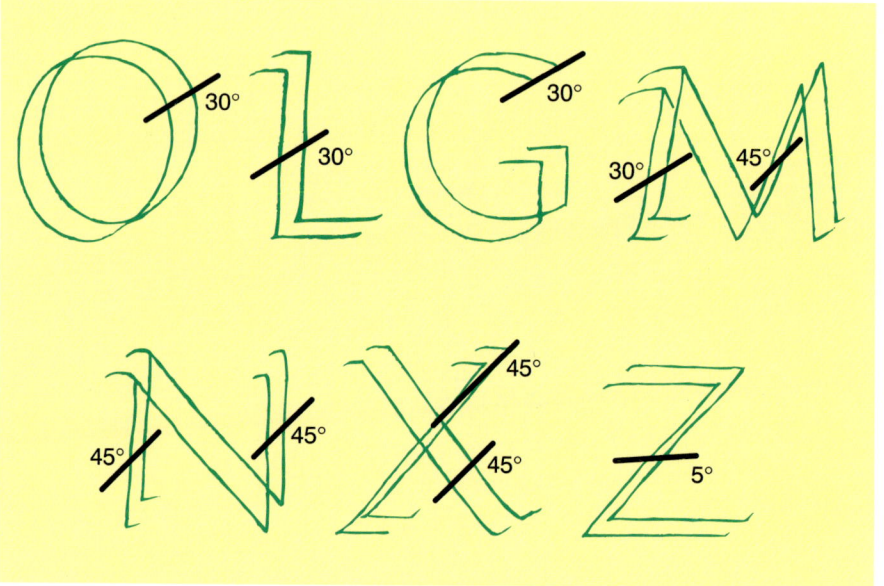

Serifs

Serifs give a finish to a pen stroke. The triangular serif (**A**) is particularly elegant; the slab serif (**B**) gives added power to a letter and is used only on capitals.

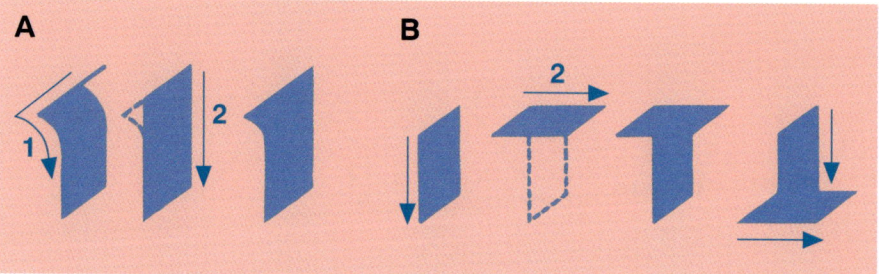

THE FOUNDATIONAL MAJUSCULES

Pen play

It is essential to feel at ease when you are learning calligraphy. As well as practising the stroke order, try some drawing with the pen. Some simple patterns based on letterforms are shown here.

lolo Ho Ho

LETTERFORMS

THE ITALIC HAND

The Italic hand was developed in 15th-century Italy during the Renaissance. Writing masters were as famous as many of the artists and craftsmen of the time, and their teaching examples are still referred to today. Italic is the most flexible of all the calligraphic hands. There are several different versions (formal, informal, pointed, cursive and chancery) and it can be compressed, extended, flourished and decorated. All Italic hands share two basic characteristics: the branching arches and the elliptical stress. It is faster to write than round hand, but concentrate at first on the shapes and the rhythm of the strokes; speed will come later.

Formal Italic

Italic minuscules have an x-height of 5 nib widths and ascender and descender heights of 8 nib widths. Italic majuscules have a height of 7 nib widths. The pen is held at a 45° angle to the writing line and all letters slant to the right no less than 5° from the vertical.

THE ITALIC HAND

Changing proportions

The Italic hand lends itself to decoration. Try increasing the height of the ascenders and descenders and adding flourishes. Remember to allow extra space above and below the x-height when ruling up if you intend to extend the height of the letters. If you are writing out a poem, or anything with more than three or four lines, keep the ascenders and descenders controlled; if they are too long and elaborate they can interrupt the flow of the piece. You will soon learn when it is appropriate to change the proportions of the letters and by how much.

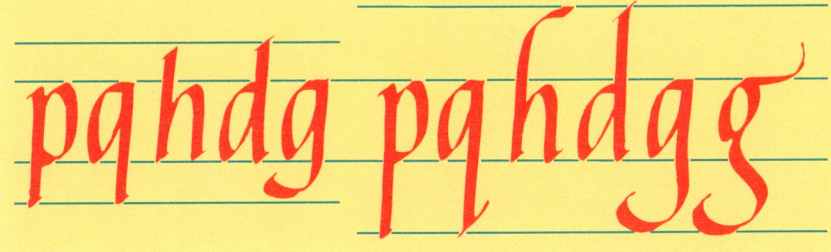

Pen play

The simple pen exercises below will give you a feel for the Italic hand.

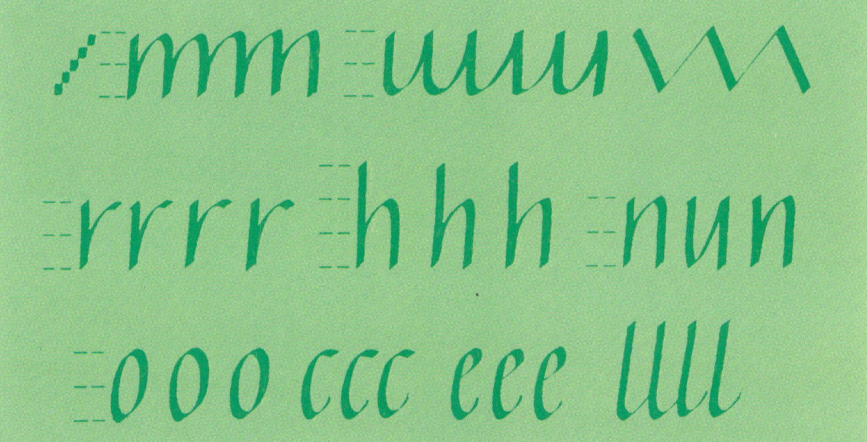

LETTERFORMS

abcdefghijklm

nopqrstuvwx

y & z g k f b A B C

THE ITALIC HAND

DEFGHIJKLMN

OPQRSTUVWX

Y&Z1234567890

FLOURISHING ITALIC

Flourishes are extensions to ascenders, descenders and capital letters, and to the last letter of a line or a word. Successful flourishes are ribbon-like, lively and a delight to the eye; flourishes done badly can be tight and condensed, or overly ornate, fussy and distracting. It is important to experiment and practise and to feel confident about making them. Start with simple ribbons and use them sparingly. As you draw the flourish, think of it as flicking a ribbon or cracking a whip, and not as an ornate pattern.

Four ways to flourish
1 On an initial letter
2 On the ascenders
3 On the descenders
4 As the finishing stroke of a word

Variations to flourishes
Examples of flourishes are shown opposite.
  A Flourishes should be free flowing and rhythmic. The exact style of flourish you choose will depend upon where the word appears in your work and the emphasis you want to put on it.
  B Overly ornate flourishes do not flow freely; they can look contrived and distract from the word. In these examples the flourishes, although ornate, are balanced by the exaggerated height of the ascenders.
  C Parallel strokes and diagonal stress give emphasis to a word.

FLOURISHING ITALIC

A

B

C

VARIATIONS OF ITALIC

Italic is a general term which covers the many variations of the Italic style. In each case, the letters are formed in the same way as formal Italic shown on pages 28 and 29, but variations are achieved by changing the letter proportions to condense or open out the letters, or by making the letters more angular or rounded.

You can see how variations can be made by writing some text with a smooth, free-flowing hand, then writing it again with the angular spiky Italic that you see at the bottom of this page. The moods of the two pieces of writing will be surprisingly different.

Decorated Italic
This Italic alphabet uses swashes – elegant, free-flowing extensions to the letters. Its letters can give vitality and charm to a piece of writing. The light and spacious quality is created by extending the ascender and descender heights of the minuscules and by opening out the majuscules. The lettering should stand on its own; do not clutter it by adding unnecessary additional decoration.

abcdefghijklmnopqrs
tuvwxyzß&&ſtABC
DEFGHIJKLM

VARIATIONS OF ITALIC

NOPQRSTUV
WXYZ

Angular Italic
This lower case Italic has an angular and spiky quality with hairlines on some ascenders and descenders.

abcdefghijkl
mnopqrstuv
wxyz &

ITALIC HANDWRITING

As you begin to develop your calligraphic skills you might like to consider ways of adapting your handwriting. Italic handwriting is a rhythmic and legible way to write beautifully all the time. Use it as often as possible, for writing cheques, notes, lists, memos, etc. The Italic handwriting alphabet is shown on pages 36 and 37. The exercises below are to help you practise the rhythmic movements that are needed for Italic handwriting. With practice, it is possible to write quickly and effectively in Italic in only a few weeks, but concentrate on shape and rhythm before attempting to increase your speed. Do not confuse Italic handwriting with formal Italic script. If you feel this is beginning to happen, stop practising one and concentrate solely on the other for a while.

Points to remember
● The x-height of the letters is 5 nib widths. The height of the ascenders and descenders is 9 nib widths. The height of the majuscules is 7 nib widths. ● Italic handwriting uses ligatures – strokes which join one letter to another to give a continuous, fluent script. For most of the time, the pen stays in contact with the paper.
● The pen should be held at an angle of 45° to the writing line to maintain the correct distribution of thick and thin lines. ● Try not to press hard with the pen; unnecessary pressure when making upwards strokes can slow you down and cause the ink to splatter.
● If you are left-handed you should use an oblique nib. It helps if you adjust the paper sideways a little and keep your left elbow tucked well in.

ITALIC HANDWRITING

35

Handwriting exercises

A 45° mountains, with thin upwards and thick downwards strokes.
B Springing arches in the proportion 2:3.
C Swinging-up pattern.
D The pull-down stroke, the arch and the ligature (joining stroke).
E Letters that can be made in one stroke: o, c and e.
F Go through the alphabet with m as a middle letter, remembering to keep the 2:3 proportion.
G Lift the pen after these letters: b, g, j, p, q, s, x, y. Lift the pen before these letters: a, c, d, g, f, z.
H Check the pen angle if your letters look wrong: (**a**) too steep, (**b**) too flat, (**c**) correct.

LETTERFORMS

a b c d e f g h i
a b c d e f g h i

j k l m n o p q r
j k l m n o p q r

r s t u v w x y z A
r s t u v w x y z A

ITALIC HANDWRITING

B C D E F G H I J

K L M N O P Q R

S T U V W X Y Z

Techniques

USING TEMPLATES

A template is a design aid. It is a basic pattern which helps you to make accurate repeats of the same shape. By using templates you can save a great deal of time and reduce the risk of inaccuracy. In this section we describe four different types of template, three of

Writing lines
These can be a very useful guide for letter proportions if you draw them to the correct sizes for your nibs. They can also be used as a guide for writing in a straight line, to measure space between lines of writing and for making up page layouts.

USING TEMPLATES

which you can make yourself. It is worth spending some time building up a range of templates. A variety of different sizes can be made very quickly using a photocopier with an enlarging and reducing facility. Once you have drawn a template, you can trace or photocopy the original and use the copies to work from. Always keep copies available so you can begin writing whenever you have a spare moment; this way you will make more efficient use of your time and achieve better results.

Plastic templates

These can be useful for drawing both regular and free flowing curves. They can be bought from art shops, but are sometimes expensive so only buy ones you know you will use.

1 Ellipses
2 Circles
3 Protractor for angles and arcs
4 Triangles (set squares)
5 French curves
6 A flexicurve (a plastic-coated wire which will bend to any shape you wish)

Pricking through and making a paper rule

When you have successfully completed one piece of work you can use it as a master copy for others by pricking through the paper with a pin at the beginning of each line. The prick marks will show on the pages underneath and can be used for ruling guidelines. Afterwards the tiny holes can be hidden by rubbing gently on the back of the paper with your fingernail. Careful examination of old manuscripts will reveal that this method has been in use for centuries. It saved time for the scribes and ensured that all the pages of a book matched. Alternatively, you can make a ruler from a piece of card and mark off the starting point of each line. The ruler can then be used as a guide for ruling up a clean sheet of paper.

USING TEMPLATES

Cutting a silhouette

A silhouette template, cut from a piece of card, can be used to help complete 'production line' projects such as Christmas cards. Accurately draw the required shape using line and shape templates. Then use the cut outline for tracing around.

TECHNIQUES

CENTRING

Centring lines of writing will immediately make a piece of work look much more professional; the effort is well worth it. Centring is traditionally used for menus and invitations, and can also be used to good effect for poems, posters and greetings cards. When setting out the lines on the page aim for symmetry of space. Centre each line according to the procedure described on the page opposite. Then experiment by moving lines closer together or further apart; it is both the look of the work and the sense of the words that will determine whether some lines should be grouped together. Complete several trial layouts; use capitals for emphasis and different nib sizes for smaller and larger letters.

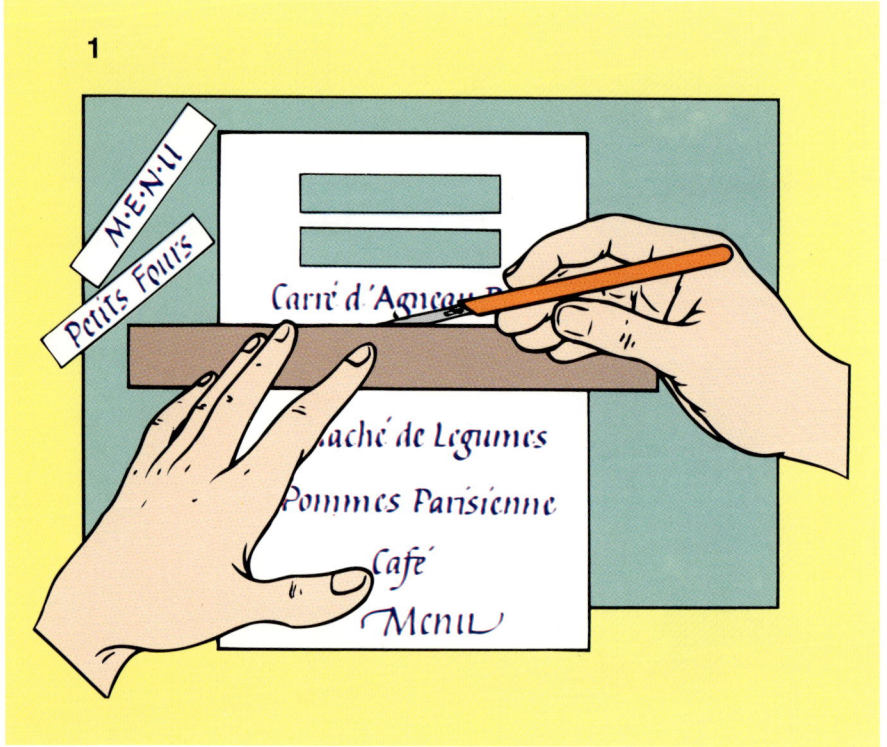

CENTRING

Procedure
- Write out individual lines of lettering several times using different nib sizes.
- Cut out the lines just above the ascenders and below the descenders. You can cut close to the capitals (**1**, *left*).
- Create a writing line template (see page 38) with a vertical line down its centre. Position the template underneath a sheet of layout paper. Use tape to fix the template and the layout paper to the drawing board.
- Measure each line of letters, marking its half-way point with a dot.
- Lay the lines of writing out in the correct order with the dots marking their centres directly over the vertical line on the template (**2**).
- Begin to experiment with the layout options. Try moving lines closer together and then further apart. Choose a layout which is symmetrical and helps to express the meaning of the words.

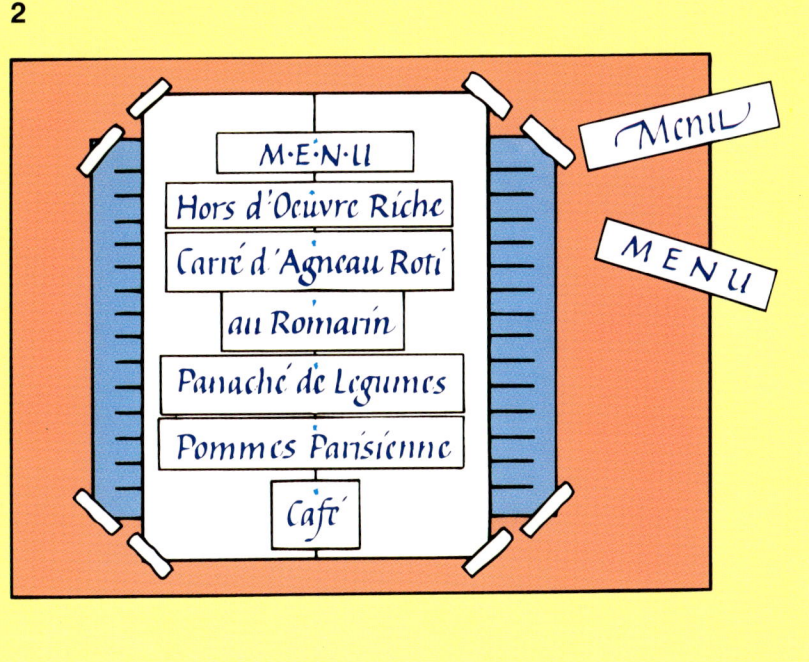

● When you think the work looks balanced, secure each piece of paper with a tiny amount of paper glue (3). Place a piece of glass over the whole paper (you could use glass taken from an old picture frame). The weight of the glass will flatten the paper and give a clearer impression of the overall effect. Make more adjustments if necessary. ● Place pieces of neutral-coloured card around the edges of the lettering (4). This will help you judge how much space to

CENTRING

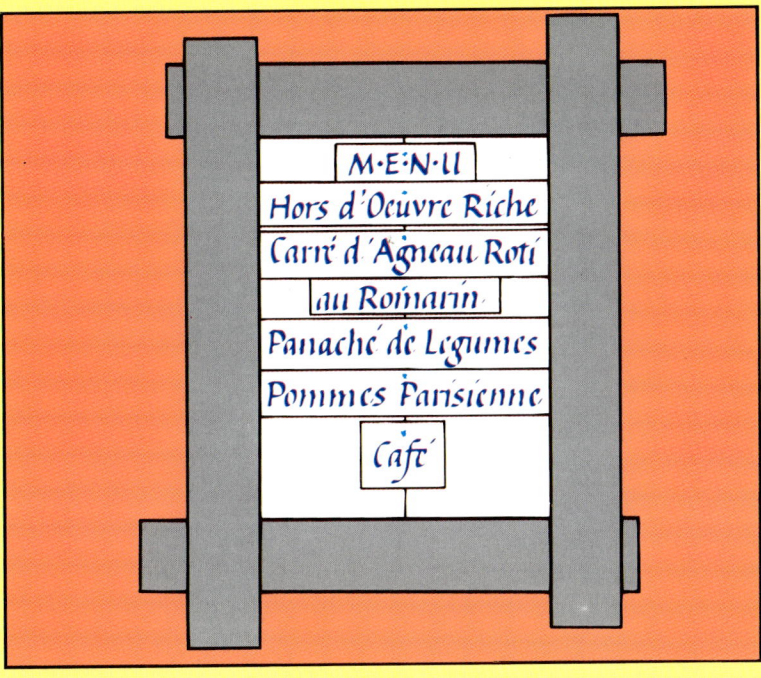

4

leave around the words. Remove the glass and mark the corner points of the layout. Create a final paste-up, sticking the labels firmly to the layout paper. ● Place the paste-up on top of a piece of good quality paper and use a pin to prick through at the ends of each line to the paper below. ● Write out the words again on the good quality paper, using the pin-pricks as guides.

TECHNIQUES

LAYOUT

Calligraphers, like actors, are interpreters of someone else's words. The work of the calligrapher should not detract from the writer's intentions and the subtleties of the piece, for example its humour, pathos or energy; ideally, it should help to express such emotions. The first and most important objective of the calligrapher is legibility – your lettering must be easy to read and the layout must be clear and easy to follow. Before you begin designing the layout read through the work and try to grasp its sense and emotion.

Interesting layouts

Collect ideas for layouts from historical manuscripts and other cultural sources. Here are some of the many variations:

1 Use space to focus attention onto the letters. This device is frequently used in Eastern art.
2 If you have a large text, try splitting it into two columns. Bibles and newspapers are often organized in this way.
3 Embellish the opening of your text with large words. This device is used in Bibles and legal documents.
4 Stagger the work quite freely. This organization would be appropriate for a humorous quotation or a lyrical rhyme.
5 and **6** Use geometric shapes to give structure and to embellish.

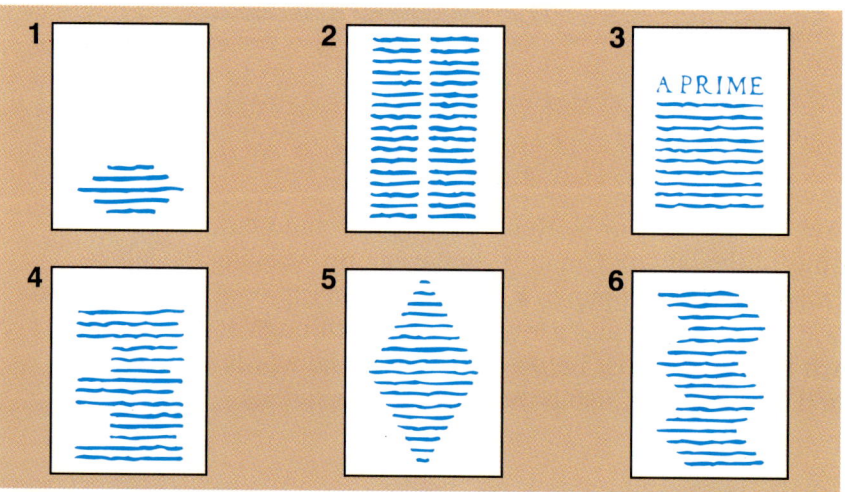